# History Happened To Me Today

Written by Savannah Brent and LaToria Brent

Illustrated by Palwasha Sajid

This book is dedicated to my family and friends.
Thank you for supporting me. Thank you for teaching me how to be kind to everyone regardless of race. Thank you to my grandparents for teaching me about history and that it can repeat itself at any moment.

Mommy, thank you for always turning bad experiences into positive ones and supporting me.

S.B.

My name is Savi which is short for Savannah, I am currently 9 years old. I love playing Roblox, computer games, with my dog, and all things science.

I am in the 3rd grade, and I really like my school. My favorite subjects are math and science. I have two sisters one is older, and a little sister who is younger than me.

Over the last year, my mom taught me the importance of treating others how you would like to be treated no matter what your race is. My family and friends are people of different cultures and race.

I would like to share my story about how History Happened to me.

One day at school during PE class, a few friends were playing a game called family. I asked if I could join the game family and play as well. It was then when Mary told me I could not play family with them because no black people are in their family. Then my other two friends, Monica and Logan, agreed with Mary saying, "Yea we have no black people in our family."

I began to cry and run away, but it wasn't over because Mary also called me stupid, ugly, and black.

Mary herself, being of minority, but from a different country, really hurt my feelings in many ways. I told the teacher, and my other friends were also crying with me.

What Mary, Monica, and Logan didn't understand was they were repeating history all over.

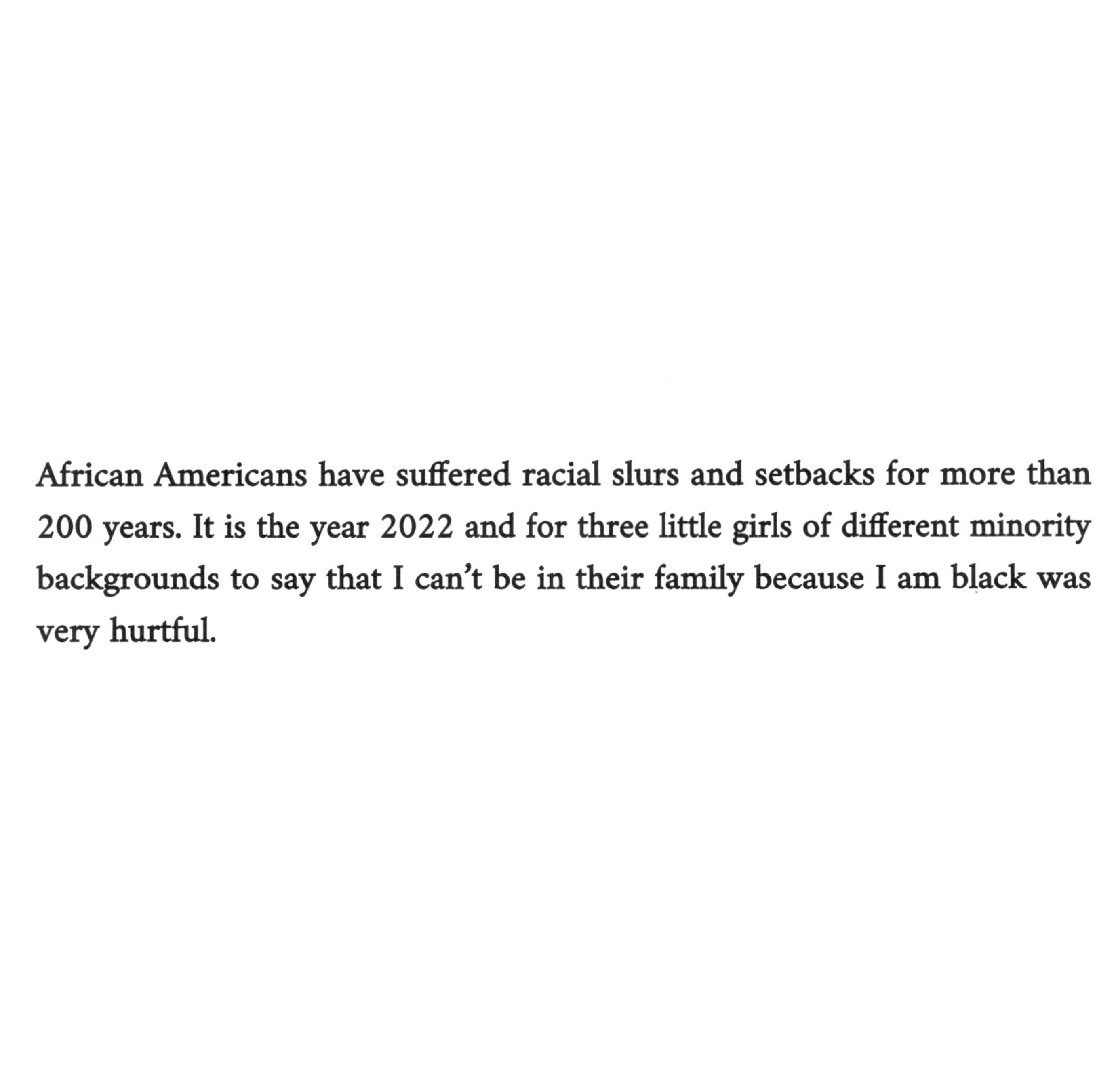

African Americans have suffered racial slurs and setbacks for more than 200 years. It is the year 2022 and for three little girls of different minority backgrounds to say that I can't be in their family because I am black was very hurtful.

BLACK IS NOT A CRIME
BLACK LIVES MATTERS
¡!/.@//!
NO

We live in a world where families look different. You have some families that have two moms or two dads that are of different racial backgrounds.

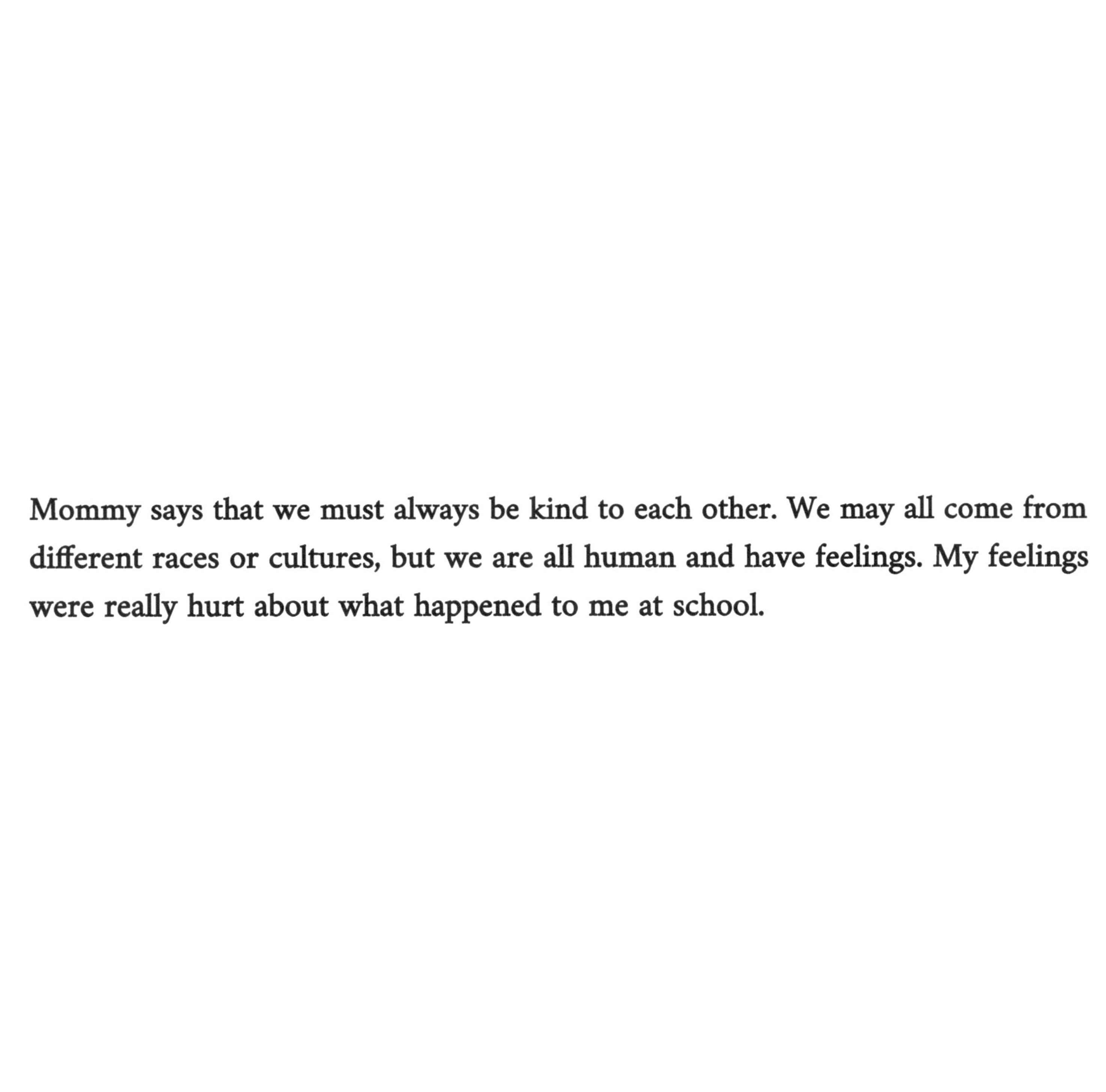

Mommy says that we must always be kind to each other. We may all come from different races or cultures, but we are all human and have feelings. My feelings were really hurt about what happened to me at school.

That evening, mommy picked me up from school. I could see the tears in her eyes, she hugged me tight as I told mommy that History Happened to me today.

Mommy told me that I am smart and beautiful, and those words that were said to me during PE were not who I am.

Once we got home, mommy read me a few bedtime stories about the civil rights moment and encouraged me to stay strong and that she would handle the situation with the school.

Mommy also gave me a few books to share with my class about civil rights and the history of black america.

Civil Rights

I hope that Mary, Monica, and Logan can understand that those words were not kind words and that we must treat each other with kindness no matter your race or culture. Remember, History can repeat itself at any moment in time. It's how you choose to handle the situation, until next time, Love Savi.

History Happened to Me today
SCHOOL

# About the Authors

Savannah Brent

Savannah has a passion for community service and helping the homeless. She loves playing video games, has a passion for science and having fun at school. In her free time, she enjoys swimming and being with family.

LaToria Brent

We hope that you will enjoy this story and encourage your family to learn about other races and cultures. We may all look different, but we are all human with feelings it is important that we teach our children about race, and how to treat everyone the same regardless of race. As, a mother of three daughters it is important that I teach my children how to treat others and to learn and embrace other races and cultures.